Hamza's Fi

MW01717334

By Gauher and Asna Chaudhry

ISBN 0-9739778-0-9
Published in Canada by iPromote Media Inc.
Printed by: www.inkwellprinting.com

One morning Hamza woke up bright and early and went to the family room and said to his brother Ali, "Assalamalakum, let's go have our breakfast."

Ali replied, "I'm not going to eat breakfast today because it's the first day of Ramadan and I'm fasting today." Hamza didn't understand the meaning of fasting.

Confused, Hamza went to the kitchen where Mama was preparing breakfast for him and asked, "Mama, what's Ramadan and why is Ali fasting?" Mama smiled. She was glad Hamza had asked and replied, "Hamza, Ramadan is a special month where Muslims don't eat or drink anything from dawn to sunset."

Mama explained how fasting is one of the five pillars of Islam and that Hamza didn't have to fast yet as he was still too young.

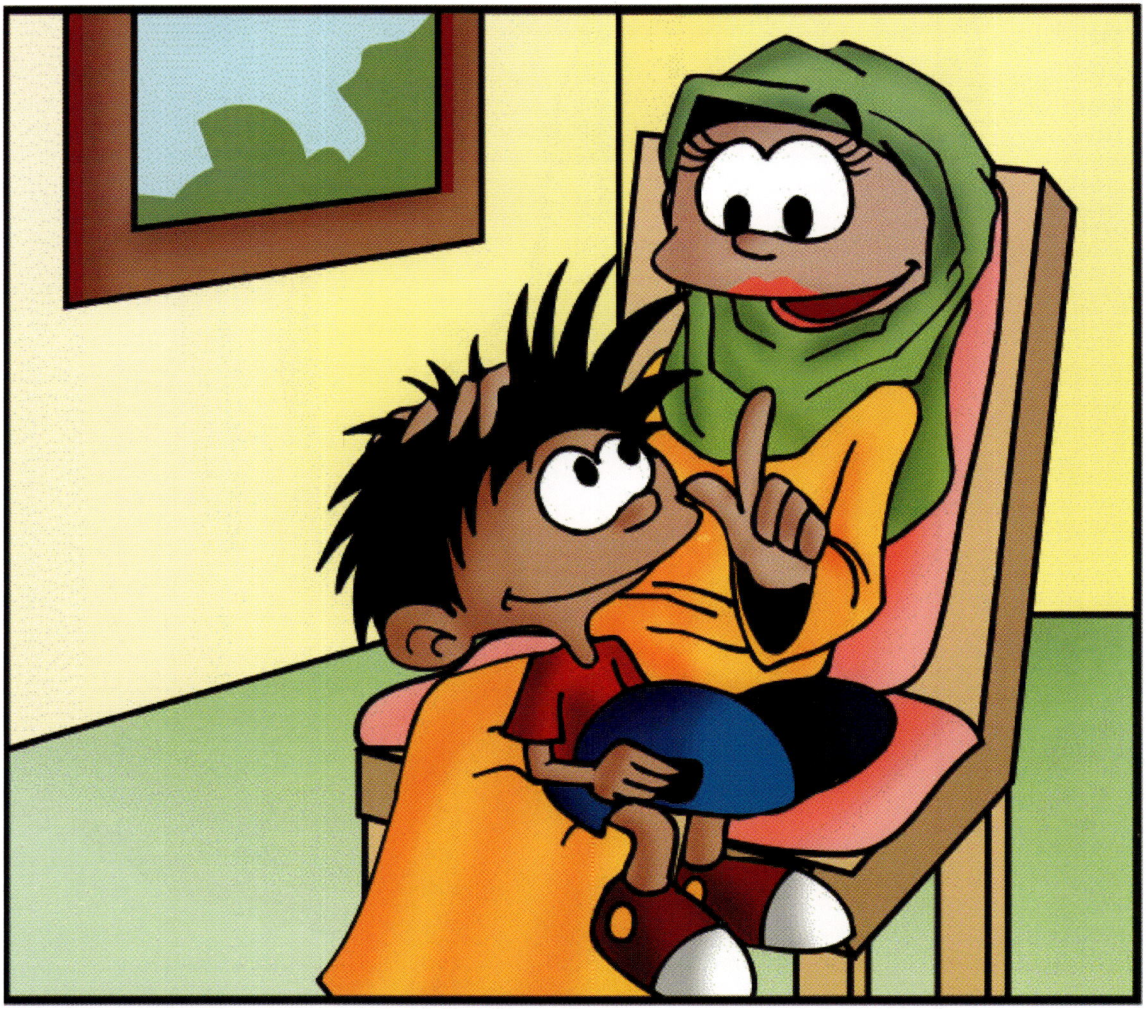

“Fasting in the month of Ramadan teaches us self-control and patience Hamza. It also helps us understand what people who don’t have anything to eat or drink feel like,” said Mama.

Hamza didn’t think he was too young to fast. He was sad that everyone was fasting in his family except for him.

At that moment Hamza got the idea that he was going to fast too! Even though Mama said he didn't have to fast, he still wanted to try. Hamza decided he wasn't going to eat or drink anything until after sunset.

He was very excited about fasting. A few hours later Hamza found his Papa and told him he was fasting too. "That's wonderful Hamza, I'm going to read my Dhuhr prayer, why don't you join me?" Papa asked. Hamza decided he wanted to please Allah. "Okay Papa, let's go and pray."

After a while Hamza started to feel hungry and went to see if his sister Aisha was also feeling hungry.

Aisha explained, "We're lucky that we're only fasting for the day. There are people in the world that don't get to eat or drink for days." Hamza felt sad. He didn't want there to be hungry people in the world.

Hamza started to think about what Aisha had said. "I wish that I could do something to help them," Hamza thought to himself.

Trying to keep his mind off of food, Hamza decided to play on his swing set in the backyard. He wondered how much longer he would have to fast.

Hamza went inside to play video games to pass the time away. But no matter what he did, he couldn't keep his mind off of food.

Time passed by slowly and Hamza started to feel really hungry. He was getting quite frustrated with the whole idea of fasting.

Hamza couldn't take it anymore! This wasn't as easy as he thought it would be. He felt he could no longer go without eating or drinking.

Hamza made a decision that he would eat a cookie. Even though Mama told him that he didn't have to fast because he was too young, he didn't want his family to know that he couldn't keep his fast. He went into his room and put on a disguise.

Making sure that no one was watching, Hamza went downstairs and quietly entered the kitchen. He slowly made his way to the cookie jar.

He managed to get the cookie jar and sneak it down to the basement. By just looking at the cookies, Hamza's mouth began to water.

Hamza was about to eat a cookie, but then started to feel guilty. He remembered that there were people in the world that couldn't eat or drink for days.

He felt lucky that he had food and water unlike other unfortunate children. Allah would also be pleased with him for fasting so he decided not to eat the cookie.

Hamza put the cookie back in the cookie jar. "I'm not going to eat the cookie, I can do this," he said to himself.

A few minutes later Hamza heard Aisha call him. It was time to sit with his family and break his fast. "Oh yes!" he said.

"Masha'Allah, Mama and I are so proud of you Hamza," said Papa. The family gave thanks to Allah and sat down and opened their fast. "You must feel really good for completing your first fast," said Ali. Smiling, Hamza replied, "I sure do."